MW01268625

By Kathleen Beharry and Reni Miller
Illustrations by George F. Kocar

Our Mission Statement

Blessing House serves as a safety net for families in crisis by providing a safe shelter for children and support for their family.

5440 Grove Avenue, Lorain Ohio 44155
440-240-1851
www.blessinghouse.org

Blessing House is licensed in the State of Ohio by the
Ohio Department of Job and Family Services as a crisis care facility.

Handprints

9 8 7 6 5 4 3 2 1

First Edition

Printed in the United States of America

ISBN 978-1-7325191-5-2

If These Walls Could Talk

If these walls could talk
Of the things that they remember...
They would tell stories
Of cherished loved ones
And rooms filled with joy
And shouts of laughter.

If these hallowed halls could share
The tale they have to speak...
Of children having pillow fights
And playing hide and seek.

If these window panes were eyes,
I guess they would have seen it all.
Each dream big enough to dream
Each little tear...Each hug...Each sigh.

If this house could share its tale
Of the lives inside these walls...
It would tell you of unfailing love
And all the memories tucked away
That's what these walls
Would have to say.

– Author Unknown

To the children of Blessing House
who have graced our lives.

———

Many Blessings

Kathleen Behary

Leaving Home

RT knew there was no reason to be afraid. He knew he had to be tough. He had moved before, and he could move again. He clutched his backpack and grocery store bag tightly. Everything he owned in the world was in those bags and he wasn't going to let anyone take them.

RT had lived with his mom after his dad left and that had been okay until she became sick and died. Then his dad had tried to take care of him but that hadn't worked out. When he was with his Nana it was a good time, but there had been a fire at their apartment building and they had nowhere to live. She couldn't take care of him until she found them a new place.

Nana had been happy when she heard about this house where he could stay. She said it was a blessing, but RT thought it just looked like an old house on a kind of busy street. Nana knocked on the door and it was opened by a kind looking woman with a big three-legged dog.

"Welcome to Blessing House," she said.

She led RT and Nana into the counselor's office where a woman was waiting to talk to Nana.

Nana gave him a big hug and told him to be good and that she would see him soon. Nana wished she didn't have to leave RT. He has been through a lot for a kid his age, but she had a good feeling about Blessing House, that it was a special place.

"Are you sure you can't stay?" RT asked.

"No, as I told you, this is a children's place and only children can stay here," Nana said. "You'll be fine, and I will see you soon."

RT had to remind himself that he was going to be tough because there were tears starting to form in his eyes.

The Lighthouse Room

"My name is Sister Mary," said the woman with the kind face. "Let's go take a look at the house." As they went down the hall, RT saw many doors. He wondered what was behind them. At the end of the hall, there was a set of stairs.

They climbed the stairs to the second floor with the big dog following behind. There were three bedrooms and Sister Mary led him into one she called the Lighthouse Room.

"This will be your room," Sister Mary said. "You are here all alone at the moment, but I am sure you will have a roommate soon."

RT put his backpack and his grocery bag on the bed and looked around the room. It was small but bright and it was all his. He almost smiled, but then he remembered that he should be tough.

"Let's go downstairs and see the rest of the house," Sister Mary said.

They went back down the stairs with the big dog still following them. It had a wonderful space for kids to play in. A group was seated on the floor in a circle playing a game with a ball.

One of the kids got mad and threw the ball at the wall by where RT was standing. RT ducked and almost fell over. The woman in the circle spoke to the child in a soft voice and he got up and went to get the ball.

"Sorry, hope I didn't scare you," he said as he walked by.

RT shook it off and said, "no problem," after all, he had to be tough.

Meeting Cassandra

A voice behind RT said, "Don't mind him, sometimes he loses control."

RT turned and looked at the girl standing next to him. She was taller than him and had a nice smile.

"Oh Cassandra, I am glad to see you. This is our newest housemate. His name is RT," said Sister Mary. "Why don't you help me show him the rest of the house?"

"OK," said Cassandra. "Let's go to the kitchen."

The big dog looked at Cassandra and at Sister Mary and decided to go with them.

"This is Moses. He is so special and he loves every one of us. He's the best dog," said Cassandra. "He lost his leg when he was younger, but he walks perfectly without it."

The four of them headed down the hall. RT suddenly stopped and stared. "Who did this?" he asked. "Did they get in trouble?"

"No silly," said Cassandra. "Everyone who comes here puts their handprint on the wall. Blessing House is no ordinary place. It's the house with the heart."

"Is your handprint here?" asked RT.

"Yes," said Cassandra. "It's right here. I was a lot smaller. Come on, I know where we can get something to eat."

Cassandra led him to the kitchen where they grabbed a snack.

When they got to the kitchen, RT thought that it was large and neat. It had the biggest refrigerator he ever saw. It was pretty cool. He didn't say anything though because if he was tough, he wouldn't care.

"Sister Mary, can we go outside?" asked Cassandra.

"Of course," responded Sister Mary.

"Let's go the park," suggested Cassandra.

"The park?" asked RT.

"Yes, that's what we call the backyard here at Blessing House. Come on, you'll see."

The Park

The backyard had a swing set and loads of toys. Over in the corner there was a group of picnic tables. Cassandra led the way and sat down at the picnic table. She opened her bag of chips and offered some to RT.

"Thanks," he said. "Would you like some of my cookies?"

RT and Cassandra sat at the table eating their snacks. When RT looked around there were lots of trees and colorful flowers along the backyard fence. He thought it looked pretty. While he was enjoying the snacks he saw several things he wanted to try, especially the monkey bars.

"So why are you here?" Cassandra asked.

RT was trying to be tough and didn't know how much he wanted to share.

"There was a fire," he said. "And I can't stay there." RT had decided he didn't want to tell her everything. He quickly asked, "Have you been here long? You seem to know a lot."

"I haven't been here long, but I have been here a lot. My brother has some health problems and needs to go to the hospital and my mom doesn't have anyone to take care of me. Sometimes I am just here for a few days and once I was here for three weeks."

Before RT could ask another question, the back door opened and the kids who had been sitting in the circle came out the door. The toys were quickly taken over and RT noticed that the boy who had almost hit him with the ball was heading for the monkey bars.

RT hesitated for a minute and then decided that there was room for two. He got up from the table. He climbed up on the bars and looked across at the other boy. The blond-haired boy looked about the same age as he was, RT thought. Neither one could think of what to say. Then suddenly, Cassandra joined them.

"Hi Max, have you met RT?" Cassandra asked.

"Hi, RT. Sorry I almost hit you with the ball. Sometimes I get angry too easily. Miss Laurie is helping me learn to be patient and nicer. Do you want to climb to the top?"

Bedtime

The rest of the day flew by and RT was surprised how much fun he had at the park with Max and Cassandra. Now it was time to get ready for bed. RT was thrilled to have the room to himself.

There was a blue tote bag sitting on his bed. When he looked inside, he found a pile of clothes with a new pair of pajamas on top. He quickly put them on and taking the toothbrush and toothpaste he found in the bag, went in search of the bathroom. He had to wait his turn, but soon he was under the covers and snug in his bed.

Miss Tamika came to the door to say goodnight.

"The alarm will ring at 7am so you can be ready for school," she said. "We have breakfast everyday so come down when you are dressed."

School? RT thought. *I didn't think I would have to go to a new school too!* But he knew he had to be tough and figured that he could do it.

As RT laid in the bed he started thinking about the day and was missing his Nana. He was surprised that today wasn't so bad and that he had fun playing on the monkey bars.

Suddenly the alarm went off. He realized that he was so comfortable here that he had fallen asleep. He took his turn in the bathroom, dressed quickly, and ran down the steps.

He was HUNGRY!

He stopped in the doorway and looked at all the kids and all the food. Eggs *and* toast *and* pancakes *and* syrup *and* fruit *and* cereal. He didn't know what he wanted. It all looked so good.

"Hey RT," Max said. "Come sit by me." RT filled a plate and sat by Max. He was happy with breakfast but still worried about going to a new school.

West Park

All around him the children were saying, "Hi, Sister Mary."

"Good morning, everyone. Did you sleep well?" she asked.

"YES!" they all yelled.

"That's good," said Sister Mary. "Now it's time for school."

Oh no, thought RT. He had to work hard to remember he had to be tough because he was scared of a new school.

"All the children that go to Erie View Elementary will go with Miss Donna today in the blue van. Those of you who go to Southeast will go with Miss Rosa," Sister Mary said.

RT realized that he didn't know which school he was going to. Then Sister Mary said, "RT, today I will be taking you to West Park with Max and Cassandra."

RT's eyes lit-up. He was going to his own school with his new friends. Wow, he had a new pair of pajamas, a great breakfast, and now he was going to his own school. Not too bad.

After school, RT went to the corner where Sister Mary told him to meet Cassandra and Max.

He thought about the day at school. He didn't see Cassandra and Max but was glad they went to the same school. The kids in his class at school weren't always nice to him, but he was seeing that at Blessing House it was different.

Cassandra and Max were already at the corner. Suddenly, the big blue van turned the corner and a smiling Miss Donna said, "Get in you three, we all came to get you today".

"Hi, RT," the kids in the van said.

Homework

When they arrived back at Blessing House there were two dogs waiting for the children.

"This is Jonah," Cassandra said. "He is our dog too."

"Let's go out to the park," RT said. "I want to climb to the top of the monkey bars again."

"Oh no, RT," said Miss Laurie. "We like to have a snack and get our homework done before we play. Do you have anything you need to do?"

"Just some spelling words. I can already do them all," said RT.

"Why don't we sit down together and try," said Miss Laurie.

"You're going to help me?" asked RT. His Nana was always too busy with dinner and things to help him.

"Of course, I will help," Miss Laurie said with a smile. As they worked on the words, RT realized that they were harder than he thought. It was really nice to have some help. When they were done, he knew his words and was sure that no one would be able to make fun of him tomorrow.

A Lot of Questions

Cassandra had finished her work also. They stopped in the kitchen to grab a snack and headed out to the park. They sat at the picnic table and looked at the other kids playing.

"Can I ask you a question?" RT said. "That nice lady, why do you all call her Sister Mary and where has she gone? Whose sister is she? And who are all the other ladies that are here?"

"Wow, that's a lot of questions," Cassandra said. "She isn't anybody's sister, she is a Nun. That's a woman who loves God in a special way and shows it by taking care of others like us. The other ladies like Miss Laurie and Miss Tamika are here to take care of us also and to help us with our homework and to learn things. Miss Donna has an important role here at the house too."

"Sister Mary isn't at the house all the time because it is hard to run a house this big. Sister Mary and Miss Donna meet with people, talk to them about Blessing House and ask them to help."

RT thought he had to be tough because he had to do almost everything by himself. *If Sister Mary needs help it must be okay,* he thought. *I guess getting help is good. Miss Laurie here helped me with my spelling and I'm going to get a good grade tomorrow.*

Cassandra offered RT a cookie. When she passed it to him, she noticed Jonah with his tail wagging, sitting just behind them. She looked at Jonah and told him to wait while she ate her cookie. Cassandra said, "Sit still," and he sat very still.

When Cassandra got to the end of her cookie, she held out the last bite and he gently took it from her hand. "Good boy, Jonah!" said Cassandra. After he swallowed his bite, Jonah looked at RT's cookie.

RT was really liking his cookie, but he decided to share his last bite with the dog. Jonah licked it right out of RT's hand. His tongue felt cold and wet. When Jonah was done, he gave RT a big doggy kiss.

RT was happy that he had shared his cookie. Now he had another new friend.

A New Arrival

Miss Laurie came to the back door and called, "RT could you come in for a minute please?" RT got up from the picnic table and went inside.

Miss Laurie said, "Come with me I have someone I want you to meet."

They walked back to the room where RT had first entered the house. A little boy was standing there with his mother.

"RT, this is Jose. He will be staying with us for a while and he will be sharing the Lighthouse Room with you," Miss Laurie said.

RT had never shared a room before and he wasn't sure he would like that.

Jose had big brown eyes like RT, and looked like he was scared. He was holding a blanket and a bear very tightly.

"RT, you and Miss Rosa can take Jose and show him your bedroom," said Miss Laurie.

Jose looked like he was going to cry when his mother gave him a hug and said, "Go with your new friend, I'll see you again soon."

Jose reached out and took RT's hand. At first, RT didn't know what to do, then he led the little boy out the door and up the stairs.

"This is our room," RT said, "and that is your bed. Come on, I will show you the rest of the house with Miss Rosa."

Jose just stood there hugging his bear.

RT stood for a minute thinking, a little uncomfortable. "It's okay," said RT, "I know how you feel. I was new too. Everybody is really nice. You can trust me."

RT stopped for a moment and thought about what he had just said. *Jose needs to trust me, and I need to trust people too!*

RT held out his hand and Jose took it. When they went down the stairs they passed through the hallway with the handprints on the wall.

Jose said, "Wow, who put all these hands on the wall?"

"My friend Cassandra told me that it's all the kids who have come to stay at Blessing House," RT said.

"Which hand is yours?" Jose asked.

"Mine isn't there yet," said RT. "Maybe we can put our hands up on the wall together."

As they were standing there, they asked Miss Rosa, "Do we get to put our hands on the wall?"

"Of course, you do," Miss Rosa said. "I'll speak to Sister Mary. Right now, why don't you boys go play in the park?"

"The park is what we call our playground at Blessing House," said RT to Jose.

The Visit

The next day when RT arrived from school, he saw Sister Mary coming towards him.

"RT," said Sister Mary, "you have a special visitor."

As RT walked to the hall, he saw his Nana. He ran to her so fast, he almost knocked her over as he hugged her ever so tight.

"Oh, my boy," said Nana. "I've missed you so much."

Sister Mary told RT and Nana that they could go outside to the park for their visit.

"How are you doing, my darling?" Nana asked.

"I'm okay. I have made some friends here Nana," said RT.

"Oh, that's wonderful. Who are they and what are their names?"

"Their names are Cassandra and Max and they go to my school. They are in a different grade."

"Cassandra has red curly hair and green eyes. She is older than me but really nice."

"Max is near my age and he's lots of fun. He told me that sometimes he gets angry real fast but he's getting better. I think he has been here for a long time."

"I won't have to stay here too long, will I Nana? It's nice here but I miss being with you."

"Not too long," Nana said. All of a sudden RT looked up and saw Jose.

"Hi Jose," RT said. "This is my Nana." To Nana he said, "I'm Jose's helper here at Blessing House. We share a bedroom."

Nana said, "Nice to meet you, Jose." Still a little unsure, Jose gave Nana a shy smile.

Nana said, "I'm so glad you have made some friends here. How are you doing at school?"

"Oh Nana, I only missed one word on my spelling test. Miss Laurie helped me study."

"Wow, that is really great. I'm so proud of you," said Nana.

Time flew by and Nana realized she had to leave and go back to the temporary place where she was living. She worked at a factory and had to be there early in the morning. It was also time for RT to get ready for bed. RT hugged his grandmother and she noticed some tears in his eyes.

"We should have a new place soon," Nana said. "Oh, here comes Miss Rosa. You be good and I'll see you before you know it."

RT took Jose's hand and went upstairs to their bedroom. Miss Rosa helped Jose get into his PJ's and RT got ready for bed too.

When Nana got to the place where she was staying, she thought about her visit with Ricky. She was so happy she had left him at Blessing House until she could find them a permanent home. *Blessing House is special.*

Blessing House has made it easier for me and seems to have helped RT in many ways, she thought. *I'm so glad he has some new friends.*

Handprints

The next day after school he saw Sister Mary at the door.

"RT," said Sister Mary. "It is time for you to put your handprint on the wall."

"Oh, great!" RT was so excited.

"Do you have a favorite color?" Sister Mary asked.

"I like green," RT responded.

"Wonderful! That's a cool color."

"Could Jose put his handprint on the wall too?"

"Of course, go find him," said Sister Mary.

While looking for Jose, he ran into Cassandra and Max. "I'm going to put my handprint on the wall!" RT shouted.

Cassandra and Max jumped up and down with excitement. They found Jose in the kitchen eating a snack.

"We're going to put our handprint on the wall," RT said to Jose. Jose's eyes lit up. "What's your favorite color?" RT asked.

"I like blue," Jose said.

"Come on, let's find Sister Mary."

They found Sister Mary in the game room. She had put on the table the paints and some paper plates and water.

Sister Mary asked Jose, "What color do you want to use for your handprint?"

"BLUE!" shouted Jose.

Sister Mary got the blue and green paints ready.

As Sister was setting up, RT remembered what Cassandra said when he first met her. He would always be a part of Blessing House, "the house with the heart." Now he understood. The handprints added to how special Blessing House was.

They saw a space at the end of the hallway, and stuck their hands in their favorite paint color. Finally, their handprints were on the wall with all the other children's. It looked so cool. He felt important and special in a way. He was really a part of something. He looked at Cassandra smiling.

Friendship &Trust

It's been two weeks since RT has been at Blessing House. He has seen kids come and go and wondered when he would be leaving to be with Nana. He was enjoying his new friends and the help from the ladies with his school work, but realized it was only temporary. Even school wasn't so bad since his new friends were there too.

The weather was rainy and all the kids were in little groups playing in the game room. RT was sitting with Max and Cassandra. Jose was coloring with the younger kids.

Cassandra looked very serious for a moment and said, "I have to tell you something. Miss Laurie told me that my brother is coming home from the hospital and my mom is coming to get me tomorrow after school."

Max and RT just looked at each other. They had never thought about what would happen when one of them left. They knew that staying at Blessing House was only temporary, but just never thought that they would lose their good friends.

That night RT had trouble falling asleep, because of Cassandra's leaving and because of his secret.

The next morning when they were in the van on their way to school, Cassandra said, "I have an idea of how we can always be friends. I will give you both my phone number and address so you can always get in touch with me."

"I can give you mine too," said Max. When they got to school, they each took a page out of their binder. They wrote their names out and their phone number and gave their information to each other.

"I can't," said RT, "because I don't know where my new home will be."

"That's okay," said Cassandra. "Once you know where your new home is, you can let us both know because you have our phone numbers. We can be friends forever and always be there for each other."

"We met at Blessing House and we have a special bond. We know all about each other."

Right, thought RT. *I guess I have to trust my friends.* "I have something to tell you. My name is Ricky Thomas. I kept that a secret. I wanted to be RT."

"When I came to Blessing House, I felt I had to be tough and RT sounds tough. After being here and meeting both of you and all the other kids, I learned that wasn't so. When you have friends, you don't always have to be so tough. I don't need to be called RT. From now on you can call me Ricky. I found out that having friends makes you stronger. They help you when things get hard."

"You are so right," said Cassandra.

Someone's Going Home

It seemed strange when Cassandra left. Max and Ricky kept each other busy playing in the game room and the park but it wasn't the same.   While in the game room, they read books and Ricky sometimes read to Jose.

Ricky helped Max with his spelling words. It made him feel important to be able to help. Max started reading to Jose and the little kids, but still they missed Cassandra.

Later in the day, Sister Mary came to see Ricky.

"I have good news. You will be going to your new home tomorrow. Your Nana will be picking you up when you get back from school."

Ricky was so happy, but also sad, because he had to tell his friends that he would be leaving.

After dinner that night Ricky asked Max to go sit at the picnic table with him. "I have something to tell you," he said. "My Nana is coming for me tomorrow and I am going to my new home."

Max looked like he didn't know what to say.

"I'm really going to miss you," Ricky said. "But remember we are friends forever. Do you know when you will be going home Max?"

"I think Sister Mary said next week," replied Max.

"Great I'll get you my number," RT said.

Leaving

When Ricky woke up the next morning, he realized that everything was going to change. He got up, dressed and then he helped Jose get ready. He had to pack his bag and get ready to leave. His backpack was full of the new clothes that had been on his bed that first night. His other things he put in the new blue tote bag.

He went downstairs to breakfast and sat with Max and Jose. Breakfast was good as usual. He had a little bit of everything. He got in the blue van with the rest of the kids and went to school. The day seemed to last forever. He didn't run into Cassandra at school, but it was a busy day. He did know he couldn't wait to see Nana and his new home.

When he got back to Blessing House, he was excited to see his Nana's car. Moses and Jonah were also waiting for him. "I'm going to miss you guys," he said. The two dogs gave him loads of sloppy kisses.

He went inside and there was Nana with Sister Mary and Miss Donna. "Are you ready to go to your new home?" Miss Donna asked.

"Yes," said Ricky, "I just have to get my things."

Coming back downstairs Ricky went to the end of the hallway where all the handprints were on the wall.

He looked at his handprint for a minute and at Jose's next to him and realized how special the wall was. He would always be here. He placed his hand over the handprint and held it there a minute. He looked at Max's and Cassandra's handprints and then walked down the hall. He took Nana's hand and they left.

Ricky's New Home

Ricky got into Nana's car. "I am so excited for you to see our new home," Nana said.

"What's it like?" asked Ricky.

"I'm not going to tell you. You just have to wait until we get there," Nana said.

They drove for just a little while and then Nana turned down a street with houses and yards. There weren't any tall buildings like where they used to live.

Nana pulled into the driveway of a little house with a nice yard. "We're here," she said.

"This is where we are going to live?" asked Ricky. "It's a house!"

"Yes," said Nana. "This is going to be our new home. Blessing House helped us find it."

Ricky jumped out of the car and ran to the front door. Nana opened it and he went in. He was surprised to see that all the furniture from the apartment had not been hurt by the fire and was all clean and in place. His bedroom looked great and the things he thought were burned were all there.

He went out to see the back yard. It had a very nice picnic table like the one at Blessing House. There were two kids playing next door on a swing set. Ricky looked at the kids and waved and they waved back.

He went back inside and asked if he could use the cell phone. He looked in his backpack and found the slip of paper with Cassandra's number and called her. He told her all about his new home and about the kids next door. Cassandra was happy for Ricky.

"I hope you make more new friends," Cassandra said.

"I hope you can visit soon," Ricky said.

"Oh, I will," said Cassandra, smiling.

Ricky hung up the phone and went to the window. He saw that the kids were still outside playing. He wanted to join them. He was ready to make new friends.

Ricky went out the back and the kids next door yelled. "Would you like to come over and play with us?"

"Sure," said Ricky. He stuck his head back in the doorway and yelled to Nana.

"Is it okay if I go next door to play?"

"It's fine," said Nana. "I'll call you when it is time to eat."

As he reached the neighbors backyard the kids said, "hello."

"Hi," he replied. "I just moved in next door. My name is Ricky Thomas."

Safe House, Safe Child

Sr. Mary Berigan SND is a cofounder and executive director of Blessing House. Blessing House serves as a safety net for families in crisis by providing a safe shelter for children and support for the family.

Since opening in 2005, Blessing House has cared for children as young as two days and as old as 12 years. Blessing House is open 24 hours a day providing immediate safety and removal from trauma for children and a placement option for parents that is voluntary. Blessing House is

licensed to care for up to 10 children at a time and since 2005 have served and cared for over 1400 children.

In addition to a wonderful staff, they have service dogs, Golden Retrievers, such as Moses and Jonah to provide comfort, care and support to the children at Blessing House. Sadly, and most recent, Moses and Jonah crossed over the Rainbow Bridge.

About the Authors

Kathleen Beharry and Reni Miller

When Kathleen moved to Avon, Ohio, she never dreamed that 20 years later she would be co-authoring a book with Reni her next-door neighbor who was to become a close friend. Both Kathleen and Reni have educational backgrounds and thru the years, each have become involved with various charities.

Kathleen, in support of Blessing House, co-authored a book, "A Bath and a Nap for Moses" which was a successful fundraiser. When a second book for young readers was proposed, Kathleen asked Reni to work with her. The subject matter came naturally since Kathleen has supported Blessing House for 12 years.

Kathleen took Reni to the house to see the wall and both were greatly affected by it. They jumped at the chance to work together on "Handprints". It truly was a labor of love.

About the Illustrator

George F. Kocar

George is a resident of Bay Village, Ohio where he lives with his wife Kathleen. He has won numerous awards for his work, has had over 50 solo shows, and has participated in over 400 juried or invitational group shows. Recently, George has been inducted in to the Artists Archives of the Western Reserve.

We believe that children have a right
to be safe in an environment that
encourages physical, emotional and
spiritual well-being.

We believe the families in crisis need
support, encouragement and connections
to positive, helpful resources.

Blessing House answers God's call to meet
the needs of children and families in crisis
by giving families hope through God's
amazing grace.